Become an Intelligent Real Estate Investor

Your Roadmap to Passive Income & Financial Freedom

BY

INVESTING MONEY & MASTERY
www.investingmoneymastery.com

CONTENTS

INTRODUCTION

Why should you read this book? In writing "Become an Intelligent Real Estate Investor - Your Roadmap to Passive Income & Financial Freedom", my intent is to cover all topics that first-time real estate investors need to know.

In this book, you'll find discussions on passive income, the basics of real estate investment, how to think like an investor, how to invest in passive income, and 22 Sources of Returns from Investment Property. You'll gain an introduction to a complete range of knowledge in profit-generation and to begin building wealth in real estate.

Alternatively, the title for this book could have been "Real Estate 101". This book is directed at everyone who intends to sample all beginner investment topics in one easy-to-read book.

This book gives in-depth knowledge regarding each of the topics discussed herein. You'll find that this is the most detailed and practical guide to starting as a real estate investor.

I strongly believe in your desire to build wealth from property, and I will never tell my readers that this wealth will come without knowledge, time, and effort. It doesn't.

It's true you can get really wealthy in real estate, but you must learn the basics, and that's exactly what this book will help you learn.

Good luck and good fortune to you.

CHAPTER 1

WHAT IS PASSIVE INCOME?

This is basically cash flow that comes in consistently, but which requires little effort to maintain. Nevertheless, executing an investing strategy for generating passive income doesn't happen overnight. Even though the idea is to eventually have an incoming source of cash flow, without moving from your seat, setting up requires quite an effort and takes some time.

There exists a number of ways to attain passive income. However, a few of these ways are valuable and have stood the test of time, like realty investment. REITs, Mutual funds, peer-to-peer lending, dividend stocks, and side hustles are amongst the several other examples of means of getting income for investors apart from realty. While diversifying your portfolio is key to success, a good place to start is real estate.

WHY CHOOSE PASSIVE INCOME FROM REAL ESTATE?

Freedom: You become your own boss when you live off passive income as a real estate professional. You live life on your own terms without anyone dictating to you the pace and calling the shots. You are your own taskmaster as well as the sole proprietor of your financial future. When you become a passive income investor, your office can be anywhere. From responding to emails from a beach while you are sunbathing, to signing important documents at a local coffee shop, you can work anywhere. If you can't find the time to do things that you love doing like partaking in your favorite hobby or spending time with your family and friends, think about joining the world of investments that generate passive income.

Time: Time becomes your biggest asset the moment you join the real estate industry. Consider it: When was the last time you heard a real-estate investor complain about not having enough time to complete A, B, or C? Never.

Amongst the greatest advantages of earning passive income is releasing your time. The best passive income schemes are the ones you can set and forget. Investing in avenues that generate passive income guarantees that you won't run from pillar to post at the end of the month in search of funds because there is cash set aside for emergencies. This doesn't mean an investment in passive income property requires no work. Nevertheless, once your property is up and running, just a little maintenance is required.

Stability: The thought of retiring, especially if you are feeling unprepared financially, can be stress-inducing and daunting. All the "what-if" situations will give you sleepless nights and can prove to be detrimental to your health in general. When you rely on your passive income assets, however, thinking about losing that full-time job you've been protecting with all your might, or that failure to seal another real estate deal won't haunt your nights and taint your spare moments. Studying and watching closely the different passive income schemes and strategies can prove to be a great educational starting point. There is the potential of leading you to research about stocks, taxes, and other investments, which upgrades your overall financial literacy.

Why would anyone invest in real estate to earn passive income? Here's a better question. Why shouldn't investing in real estate to generate passive income be your goal?

GUIDELINES FOR INVESTING IN REAL ESTATE FOR GENERATING PASSIVE INCOME

1. IDENTIFY YOUR GOAL.

For a first-time investor, recognizing your goals will be essential to your success. What do you stand to gain? Are your dreams realistic? Are these goals lifestyle or financially driven or maybe both? If you are planning on taking passive income seriously, ask yourself if you are planning on living solely off these investments or you are planning on using the monthly profits and payments to supplement an already steady income you have. Second, how deep would you like to be involved? You might consider getting the services of a property management company to handle everyday tasks. The property management route is capital intensive, have this at the back of your mind. Clarifying your intentions before getting into the investment process is compulsory for fresh investors.

2. ORGANIZE YOUR FINANCES.

Assessing your finances is important, before making any investment. The best start is looking at your overall financial profile. What do you have for assets? Do you have a decent credit score? To acquire that new property, would you need to get a loan? Have you saved enough to avoid paying for private mortgage insurance(PMI)? What amount are you willing to put down? If necessary, would you think about talking to a private money lender? How much do you hope to receive from this transaction? Setting these questions straight and providing real answers to them would help you avoid hassles you might encounter in future.

3. DECIDE ON INVESTMENT TYPE.

From the moment you've made up your mind about investing in passive income, what comes next is determining the type of property you will like to invest in. So many options are available for new investors: Single-family homes, multifamily homes, apartments, and commercial real estate are just the start. Single-family homes carry the lowest risks but they are likely to produce lesser cash flow when compared to other real estate types. However, single-family homes have a more appreciation potential. Apartments and multifamily homes can be profitable. Investors, however, will have to bother about evictions and vacancies more often than they would in a single-family home. Investing in commercial real estate requires a huge amount of capital, but it also has a potential of giving investors huge returns in the long run. If you have the power to cover the holding cost and the first investments, commercial real estate can deliver enormous cash flow and appreciation potential. Don't forget, the kind of property you choose will be directly related to the kind of tenants you will attract, and the amount of energy you are ready to put into the establishment.

4. CHOOSE YOUR MARKET.

Investing in real estate gives option for investment in properties across the country. If, where you reside, the market doesn't offer enough ROI (return on investment) potential, think about working with a property management company and a realtor to secure a deal that is sited in a more favorable position. During research on the trends in various markets, make sure you focus on key factors such as population data, economic indicators, and housing data. Population data, like the rate of migration, past and projected job growth, and changes in population in surrounding cities, also helps in determining if a market is ripe for realty investing or not. Low unemployment rates predicted economic growth, and a low cost of living are all economic indicators. Housing data factors that investors should be aware of before selecting their market are median home prices, increasing average rental rates, property appreciation, and low vacancies.

5. DETERMINE YOUR PROPERTY'S EXPENSES AND CASH FLOW.

From the point you have a business plan, reviewed your finances, selected a market, and chosen a potential property, the next thing to do is to calculate all expenses in order to know your expected cash flow. It's as simple as this: the more research you conduct, the more accurate your projections will be. Talking to other landowners and investors, in that market or area, is a good place to start. Ask questions like, what's the cost of rent? How frequently do you face maintenance issues here? What difficulties do you face on a regular basis? Go through common rental property prices like loan interest, utilities, taxes, maintenance, insurance premiums, repairs, etc. Although a number of rental spaces are tax deductible, don't forget to calculate your total projected costs. This helps in estimating your monthly cash flow. From the moment you run the numbers across different properties, use the average results you've collated in order to establish a single unit's cash flow.

6. DECIDE THE NUMBER OF UNITS.

The easiest step is the last one. Let's say your aim is to generate $5,000 of income every month. Apply this formula: number of units needed=(equals) $5,000/(divided by) expected cash flow of one unit. Establish your expected cost of one unit, choose the income you desire, and use the formula above to know how many units you'll need.

HOW MANY RENTAL PROPERTIES SHOULD I OWN?

A perfect reply to this question will have a range and depends on each investor's specific target. Is your target to secure enough passive income properties to guarantee financial security after retirement? Are you planning on buying a property and holding onto it for a couple of years before selling it off to make a lump sum profit? Are you hoping to generate a cash flow equal to your current earnings? Are you planning on taking part in realty exit strategies like rehabbing or wholesaling? Or are you seeking to diversify your investment portfolio? Since every investor has a different reason or target, they would have a different answer to the question of the number of rental properties they should own. Some entrepreneurs own a few passive income properties just to supplement income from a full-time job; others own more than 50 properties in complete rental property investment. Return to step one and recognize your goal before revealing the solution to this question. Realize early that it is okay for your goals to change with time, but initiating an action plan to begin will help you get started.

CHAPTER 2

WHY INVEST IN REAL ESTATE?

Why should you invest in real estate? After all, there are numerous different ways to earn more money in life. The Internal Revenue Service which is the foremost authority when it comes to personal finance released statistics that disclosed that the highest percentage of personal wealth of taxpayers in the US is held in real estate.

Have you ever thought of being your own boss, running your own business, or calling the shots every time? Has it ever crossed your mind? The most likely way for any individual to become wealthy independently in one's lifetime as pointed out by the IRS is through owning your own business and entrepreneurship. Countless hours can be spent by opportunity seekers carrying out research on the best means to make money. You can end your research now if you are one of them. By becoming a real estate entrepreneur, you are provided with the highest probability for economic prosperity.

Real estate is the IDEAL investment for making money.

INCOME

With real estate, you can be provided with a steady, tax-advantaged income, often called cash flow.

A tenant can rent real estate. Over time, your mortgage can be offset by rental payments from the tenant, pay for any property management and maintenance costs, and can additionally leave enough for you to have a consistent income. Bonds and stocks that give interest and dividends are other investments that provide a consistent income. However, as compared to bonds or stocks, real estate typically provides a larger measure of income and has more tax advantage.

DEPRECIATION

This term is used for tax purposes and is of extraordinary value to people that invest in real estate. Think of a T-shirt's life span to demonstrate the concept of depreciation. It deteriorates after it has been worn and washed for several years. The average T-shirt likely lasts a few years although you may have T-shirts that have lasted decades. To determine the amount of taxes you will pay on your real estate investment, the IRS understands that a property's structure (not the land, only the structure) deteriorates too, and the life span of a residential rental property is set at 27 ½ years. Does a house that is well-maintained simply crumble to the ground after 27 ½ years? Of course not. But for deciding the amount you will be paying the IRS, whatever you purchased the property for (the land subtracted) can be depreciated over 27 ½ years.

For instance, you purchase a single-family home for $100,000 and the land is worth $10,000. That implies that for tax purposes, your tax basis (how much you purchased the structure for) is $90,000. You get a tax deduction of $3,272.73 each year for depreciation when you divide $90,000 by 27 ½ years. In the event that the cash flow of the same single-family home is positive at $270 per month or $3,000 per year, you get the opportunity to add some more depreciation expense to that property for $3,240 and therefore, in this instance you don't need to pay any income taxes on the monthly $270 you were bringing in! This is the way in which real estate rental income is incredibly tax advantageous.

For what reason would the government continue to permit this deduction for real estate investors with all the tax increment and unfair taxing rules? The government provides individuals with an incentive to be real estate owners. They want you to invest in real estate.

EQUITY

You have the chance to buy a property at a value lower than its market value when you purchase real estate. When you get a great deal, the difference between what you purchased it for and what it is worth is referred to as equity. The old saying, "In real estate, you make your money when you buy," applies in this situation.

You get equity instantly when you purchase property well below market value.

By comparison, publicly traded stocks are bought at market price. The market might be overvaluing or undervaluing the stock at the time of purchasing it, but in any case, at the exact moment a stock is bought, the amount paid is what the market will pay for it. In real estate, however, you can purchase a property at a value lower than the market value and literally turn around and sell that exact property again for tens of thousands of dollars more some minutes later.

APPRECIATION

In the last hundred years, residential real estate has kept up with inflation. The values of residential property have even appreciated above and beyond inflation in some locations. For investors that are educated and insightful, appreciation is not the reason to purchase property; it is an added financial bonus to being a real estate owner.

Purchasing real estate on the basis of the other factors listed earlier is a good decision than betting on when or if a property will appreciate since predicting the future has proved to be a hard task. Real estate appreciation can only be benefitted from if you own it. Hence, owning as much real estate as possible, as smartly as you can, will give you the best probability of gaining from appreciation. And be thankful if it comes your way.

LEVERAGE

Leverage is being put to use when you borrow money to purchase real estate. The individuals and companies of this world that control most of the money, such as mortgage companies, banks, mutual funds, hedge funds, insurance companies, pension funds, and private individuals, want to lend you money to purchase real estate. A number of them make their money by lending money to you for buying real estate.

Different types of real estate lenders exist, from those that need good credit, a great amount of money, and an extraordinary loan application, to those who just lend money against real estate depending on the property's market value. If you purchase a $100,000 property and you put down $10,000 for instance, you are utilizing leverage to own a $100,000 property with just $10,000 of your own cash. The use of leverage is the ability to borrow money to purchase real estate and it enables you to purchase more real estate with less cash.

Truly, real estate is the IDEAL investment. Of the numerous reasons real estate is so attractive, this is just one. There are numerous other reasons why investing in real estate may just be what you have been searching for in an investment vehicle or business opportunity.

There is no age, background, or ethnicity discrimination in real estate. You're not too young or too old (however, you must be 18 years old to own property). Regardless of where you are from, your age, or your nationality, you're on a level playing field with every other person.

No resume is required for real estate investing. Where you went to school, the number of jobs you've had, the lack of professional skills or skills you may have, or your resume paper's texture and color don't matter. Successful investors come from all walks of life. If you do not possess higher levels of education, you are not inferior. My mentor never attended college. Having a college or post-college degree is not a handicap either. No matter what your resume looks like, everybody is on a level playing field.

The use of your cash or credit is not always involved in purchasing and selling real estate. In this book, there are a number of strategies that you will learn that will enable you to not only make fast money but in addition, own real estate for long-term wealth accumulation without having to pay or borrow any money. An investor will certainly have more approaches to have real estate investments when he/she has cash and/or good credit, but there is a possibility for you to begin from absolute zero economic standing.

Going by the saying, "Every individual needs a roof over their head," real estate is an essential human need. This book will concentrate on real estate investing. From single family homes, to duplexes, condos, co-ops, townhomes, apartments and much more, living quarters come in all shapes and sizes as well. Unlike other various businesses and investments, real estate makes a provision for something that absolutely every individual needs which is shelter.

Real estate exists everywhere, including where you live. A typical misconception beginners have is that investing in real estate does not work in my area. That does not make any sense! Opportunities exist right under your nose. In your own backyard, diamonds exist. As a matter of fact, you will be stunned at how much money you can earn dealing real estate right in your own community once you learn and apply the methods and strategies described in this book. You have been driving by opportunities for real estate daily, believe it or not.

Whether close to home or far away, you can make real estate investments. You are not confined to only your territory. You have the ability to purchase and sell real estate anywhere although we recommend that beginners start in an area they are extremely familiar with.

Disclaimer: This book will concentrate on methods that work in Canada and the United States. Other than these two countries, I'm not acquainted with investing in in real estate. These same principles should however apply.

You can make cash in up and down markets. At the point when the real estate market is up, specific methodologies work extremely well and then in down markets, other techniques turn out to be more productive. You can attain success in real estate investments regardless of the market.

When it comes to equipment to get started, becoming a real estate investor does not require much. If you own a computer, a printer, and a telephone, you have all the equipment you need to start. In fact, you can work from your home, a café, or even your truck! Compare this to setting up other various businesses that usually require business space, a lease, staff, inventory, equipment and so on.

Launching a real estate investing operation is far easier than setting up most other businesses with almost the same level of monetary rewards. It doesn't need a board of directors, venture capital, or even a detailed business plan. As a matter of fact, your investment plan could be outlined on a napkin.

Investing in real estate doesn't require your full time. You can invest in your spare time. You may start to enjoy it so much that you want to venture into it full time after some time, but it's not necessary. In other words, investing in real estate doesn't require you to quit your day job. The limited free time you have available can be used to invest.

Moreover, perhaps the most vital consideration to most individuals, real estate can make you extremely rich as well as provide the lifestyle you have always desired. Many on the list of the world's richest individuals made their wealth in real estate.

Many of the individuals with the biggest houses in your vicinity made their money or are able to maintain their wealth from real estate. Many of the individuals you also meet on the street who are free financially have a real estate background.

You might ask, "So if real estate is so great, how come everybody isn't doing it?" That is a very good question. Real estate has a few hindrances-to-entry (a fancy business term to depict what makes a business hard for competitors to break into).

Similar to any business, investing in real estate requires very specific knowledge. This specific knowledge is rarely taught in schools. Most individuals are simply not aware of how to be a real estate investor. Also, the education process requires both application and study. Similar to chemistry in high school, where you took the lectures and afterward learned at the laboratory, investing in real estate requires both absorbing educational materials as well as the application of what you learn, and experiencing it in reality. A few concepts and ideas can rarely be acquired just by reading about it. You need to get out there and gain the experience by putting the concepts and ideas into practice.

Patience is required of anybody who makes an investment in real estate. Our world today is obsessed with instant fulfillment and paybacks. An immediate financial gain isn't guaranteed in real estate. Normally, your hard work today repays you several months after. Most partially-committed financiers pull the plug a couple of days from a massive return. I have witnessed this phenomenon multiple times in my experience. Most people just lack that patience to see their investments in real estate produce massive financial gain.

Venturing into the real estate world translates to starting your own business. Like any entrepreneur would tell you, monetary remunerations from businesses are gotten from results. This is a far cry from the way people receive compensations in jobs based on any activity measured in terms of time, be it hourly, daily, weekly or monthly. Business executives receive their pay based on how their businesses perform in the marketplace. There exists a difference in the mode of thinking between prosperous entrepreneurs and regular salary earners.

The greatest setback, for most people today, in starting their own business is never the physical challenge of completing their tasks, but the mental trouble of rewiring their minds to reason like productive business owners. Henry Ford once said, "Thinking is the hardest work there is, which is why so few people do it." Therefore, it really is important to think as investors do. The next chapter is devoted to this topic.

The greatest vehicle anyone could use to produce financial prosperity is real estate. To take advantage of the many opportunities real estate hands to you, one must possess the right education and must have wired their brain for productive real estate ownership. Some other parts of this book will be devoted to providing more knowledge with regard to these two aspects of real estate; possessing an investing mindset and drilling yourself in the particular areas that would lead you to prosperity.

CHAPTER 3

HOW TO THINK LIKE AN INVESTOR

During my early years of teaching real estate investing to new investors, I usually skipped over the mental aspect of the investment and went straight into the heart of real estate. It was a mistake!

I discovered that educating people on the techniques of real estate investments was actually very straightforward. From the moment they had the information on the steps to take, the difference between success and failure depended on what was going through their head.

Possessing all the information about investing will be of no use unless your head is clear. You will have to think like a real estate investor before being one. Your brain is a very powerful tool, but it's rather unfortunate it doesn't come with an instruction manual.

This chapter is the instruction manual you need on how to operate your brain in order to succeed as a real estate tycoon.

YOUR WHY

Why comes before what. Why you choose to do something is of more importance than what you choose to do. Humans get easily excited about new endeavors. The moment the excitement wears off, however, we tend to move on to something else. The greatest achievements in life never happened overnight. In reality, it is usually the opposite.

The greatest victories probably took some time to achieve, correct? Investing in real estate is no different. At the point the excitement wears off and the newness of real estate fades away, what can give you a reason or reasons for venturing into the world of real estate investments?

The moment I started, I desired to work from anywhere, be my boss, call the shots, earn what I believe I deserved, make lots of money, and stay financially free. Was that too much to ask? On my job, I showed up at the office, wasn't free to work anywhere, I had no control whatsoever over my time, I took instructions from the boss, I wasn't earning what I deserved, I wasn't making lots of money, and I wasn't financially free. My earnings were my only salary and the only way that could improve was by hoping for a raise. These reasons were strong for me when I began. I refused to return to that life again and that motivated me to succeed.

Why do you choose to be a real estate investor? You are in a similar situation as I was when I started? Maybe you are happy with your job and simply have decided to invest your hard-earned savings in an investment with greater returns than you are currently receiving. You might be concerned that your current financial status will not cover you properly after retirement. Do you need more time with your loved ones? Do you need more money? Do you desire freedom to see the world through traveling and exploring while you enjoy your life? Your why is your reason for becoming a real estate investor.

For your why to be effective, it must be very emotional. These emotions drive our behavior. Harnessing this power enables us to achieve extraordinary feats, far beyond what you believe is possible. The best part of finding your why is that the motivation you will ever need is already in you, instead of relying on others for motivation. Just discover what your why is in order to unlock an unlimited resource of power.

You are searching for what is absent in your life that should be present. This could be positive or negative. You may be dreaming of living every day in a tropical paradise, relaxing in a hammock in the midst of two trees while cooling from a gentle island breeze. This thought creates significant motivation within you for creating that life you desire.. What could be more important to you right now is staying away from indebtedness and raising funds for your children's college. Those feelings of pain from not being free from debt and not possessing the wealth to pay for your child's college education may weigh heavily on you. These negative emotions may act as a huge motivating factor too.

It is a fact, psychologists say, that negative emotions push us harder than positive ones. People will be more motivated to quit their jobs than to labor towards a goal of financial freedom. Bend this knowledge to your advantage first by thinking about every part of your life you never like which you believe venturing into the world of real estate could solve. Your why being very negative and emotional can be all the motivation you'll ever ask for in order to succeed in real estate.

Taking a moment, write down your why. A more emotional why gives you a greater outcome. Burn this need inside you every time you think about it. Your frustrations with how your retirement fund investments are performing along with the mere thought of how the lack of brilliance in your results gets you boiling mad, could do the trick. It could be that you are unable to be with your loved ones almost as often as you would love to because of your present financial status. If nothing comes to mind now, spend time every day for the next couple of weeks thinking of it until you find it.

In the absence of a why, there are chances that you may not take the actions important to becoming a successful real estate tycoon. It's that vital. When someone is absolutely comfortable, they hardly have strong enough reasons to do something different from what they are already doing. Knowing your hot buttons, what really makes you uncomfortable about your current scenario is the easiest and fastest way to having and maintaining consistent motivation. There is need to find your why. Make this your first task for going into real estate investment."

PAIN AND PLEASURE

There exist two basic motivating factors in our lives, pain and pleasure. We decide to do something either for the pleasure it gives us or because of the pain we believe we could prevent by taking that action. For instance, your why may be the need to fulfill that ambition of living your days on the beach with the sand and the sun. This illustrates doing it for pleasure. Alternatively, your why could be that you don't want to remain in poverty anymore. That illustrates wanting to avoid pain. This concept is simple, we know, but this is exactly how the brain works.

Applying this simple yet very powerful ideology opens up a new world for you. You learn to motivate yourself in more than a thousand ways through pain or pleasure. For instance, some of the new entrepreneurs wrestle with the paralyzing effects of fear. They are scared of talking to a motivated seller, getting a contract signed, asking for nonrefundable urgent money from a buyer, and so on. The complication here is that there are so many pieces of advice centering on thinking positive. Just thinking positive can sometimes push you to disregard fact in an attempt to eradicate fear. It's needless to turn a blind eye to the grim realities of life. Fear could be a useful factor to us, on the contrary. Fear becomes a great counselor and an excellent guide.

Instead of eradicating fear, you could use it as a motivating factor. Don't you think? Instead of worrying about, "what do I say to this homeowner," allow fear to motivate you into believing, "if I don't call this person, it could cost me $30,000 and that would absolutely devastate me plus I need that money." Preventing pain is a much stronger motivator than making efforts at gaining pleasure. People fight much harder to retrieve $20,000 someone stole from them than to save up in bits until it reaches $20,000 in their bank accounts. The drive to avoid pain is far greater than gaining pleasure. Arm yourself with this knowledge since it motivates you into taking action.

Precisely, when you strike a juncture in your investing journey, when fear starts to slow you down or paralyze you, start thinking immediately about the things you stand to lose if you do not take action. Think deeply about it until you begin to feel the pain which occurs when you refuse to take action. For instance, for some beginners, and sadly for some seasoned investors too, asking for nonrefundable, earnest money from buyers could be very nerve-racking and scary, even when it should never be. The irony is, the moment an investor gets burned once by a buyer who walks out from a deal and leaves the investor hanging, that investor would never be concerned about demanding nonrefundable earnest money.

There is a way to use the power of avoiding pain to push a new investor into getting nonrefundable earnest money from a potential buyer. They can hold this conversation in their head, "If I don't demand non-refundable earnest money from this buyer, I will potentially allow this buyer to back out of the deal scot-free and that will cost me $37,000 as well as the time I have spent getting this deal to where it is, not to mention hurting the homeowner who is counting on me to help him". That is the way to use fear and pain as drivers to assist in taking the initiative. Instead of ignoring fear and pain, take charge of the emotions and allow them to turn your life around.

YOUR COMFORT ZONE

Do you know someone who knew exactly what to do but simply refused to do it? Could that person have been you, maybe, sometimes? If that was so, could you explain why you fell into a trap of inactivity when you completely knew what you were meant to do? The answer lies somewhere in that space between your ears.

You linked pain to that major step so that although you knew how to do the chore, you didn't do it just because your brain couldn't let you do it. Our brains work in such a way whereby both positive and negative feelings are linked to our thoughts. Labels of "pleasure" or "pain" are being persistently attached by your mind to each action you take.

For instance, property sellers are in the best position for many new real estate investors to talk to. Many new investors will take part in the following scenario, rather than speaking with the owner right away to understand the person's views.

They drive to the house, inspect the outside of the home, look around and examine the neighborhood, go back home, and lastly, do all manner of online research about the property all before even speaking with the property owner.

The worst part is that the property owner's demands may be too high, or they may not even want to sell their property. All the time and energy invested as well as the travel expenses thus go to waste. Picking a phone to ask a few simple questions from the property owner would have fixed the problem instead of wasting time, energy, and money. This implies the person clearly prefers wasting time, energy, and money to making a simple phone call. People will do more than this to stay away from pain than to gain pleasure.

To buttress the example cited above, a phone conversation with the property owner is one thing that is out of the person's comfort zone. Driving around and doing online research were both well within their comfort level. You have to continually step out of your comfort zone if you want to keep being successful in life.

YOUR COMFORT ZONE AND YOUR MONEY ZONE WILL ALWAYS BE EQUAL.
Comfort zone for each person is different. Perhaps, if the person could not drive a vehicle or was unable to navigate the internet, then a phone call would have been far comfier than the two.

If your comfort zone does not include the activities described in this book, then you would have to step out of your comfort zone. This may then include improving your communication skills over the phone, using computer to set up your business online, and so on.

You have to be ready to stretch yourself. Be always ready to step out of your comfort zone. Why? That why comes here again. If you know your why, you should have the answer of the question of why stepping outside of your comfort zone is crucial. Moving from activities that are not within your comfort zone to more activities outside your comfort zone is important for you to experience your biggest breakthroughs.

ATTITUDE

Real estate investors who are ultimately successful have a unique attitude toward life. Such people do see every experience as a test and every result as a learning lesson. This results in a state of mind that does not acknowledge failure. It never produces phrases like, "Well, that was a waste." An investor with the right attitude does not waste any idea. All experiences are tests, and all results are lessons.

However, pleasant and positive emotions are not always initiated by this attitude. At times, the lessons learned by successful investors are painful and despite all the pain, they do not turn a blind eye to the pain. They experience it so that they do not have to learn the lesson again. Do not immediately believe a test is bad if you did not get the result you anticipated. This may be discouraging and not pleasant at the moment, but you may later realize that the lesson you learned was extremely worthy and essential for you to close the coming deal.

Successful investors are grateful to have the chance to invest. They have an attitude of gratitude and show gratitude for the lessons they learned and the experiences they gained. When problems arise, they don't complain. They rather see them as challenges and view such situations as opportunities to learn.

ACTION OVER ANALYSIS

The fear of the anonymous, the fear of making an error, and the fear of moving outside of their comfort zone do not allow many people to take action meanwhile the fear of not taking action at all should be their priority. We should know everyone makes mistakes when they first start a journey, and mind you, the more errors you commit, the faster you learn. So, your utmost fear should become inaction. In fact, for most successful investors, their only regret with regard to real estate business is not starting sooner.

Doing continuous analysis to the point of paralysis is a very common habit among new investors. Instead of taking action, they analyze and analyze until they are paralyzed. This arises from the fear of committing errors. Instead of taking up a deal or purchasing a property, they prefer reading several books and attending several seminars. They believe they must wait until they know much and have enough confidence to start investing. Meanwhile, in reality, these intending investors will never get to a level of knowing so much on real estate to be really confident until they take action. You tend to gain confidence when you take action rather than reading a book.

If you intend not to have only a short-term achievement in real estate, you must educate yourself regularly. Meanwhile, you must not just educate yourself; you must be taking actions too. Investors must learn new techniques and new ways of investing. In real estate, a point of total understanding of all the aspects cannot be attained. Therefore, waiting to have total confidence before taking a step will paralyze the person forever. An action is far more powerful than analysis. This is exemplified when an investor who is not afraid to try new things but with less knowledge gives a far better and faster result compared to an investor with less action and much more knowledge.

COMMITMENT

Success is always a result of long-term dedication. All successful real estate investors in the world have one thing in common that they stick with their job until they accomplish it.

You must be ready to make an earnest and binding commitment to stick with it until you succeed so as to make sure you attain your goals. You should try to always have positive thoughts which will help you succeed in life. You should be determined not to quit real estate work until you succeed. The key word in that sentence is, "until." That's what is called commitment.

In a world of starters, you will want to be a finisher. Do re-examine after attaining success in your effort. This is how successful people think. They tell themselves, "I will continue to do this until I succeed", then I can re-examine.

If you want to become a successful real estate investor, make a commitment right here, right now, and stick to it until you are successful. Fortunately, you are on the road to greatness if you can make this commitment to yourself, your family, and your future.

After reading this book, you can start putting this new commitment into use.

POSSIBILITY THINKING

Successful investors know a deal won't work due to many reasons, and when they detect at least one reason why the deal will work, the real big money is made. This is called possibility thinking. Do not stand on why things won't work, rather think of how it can work. Instead of thinking positive, which can neglect reality and literally stop growth, possibility thinking includes analyzing the cold, hard facts of a situation and thinking of creative ways to sort it out. Here's a quick way for your possibility thinking muscle to be developed. When negotiating or making a decision with another person next time, avoid using the word "no," and instead, replace with, "yes, but." This will make you start thinking skillfully, and you will be able to come up with other ways to solve problems. You must always think in terms of possibilities if you want to be a successful real estate investor.

Any transient roadblock one may encounter in real estate investment will be much like the fence. It can be overcome because the ability to overcome it is in you. A simple four-foot fence cannot stop you from freedom. You should know that.

REPETITION

For you to be good at something, you must do it over and over again... Even if you learn quickly, or you retain new information easily, repetition is still the key to mastery.

Reading the same information over and over again can be noticeably enlightening. In addition, as your view transforms, you will see concepts and ideas that you never noticed before.

After reading this book, apply the skills and methods you learned repeatedly. At the end, they will get embedded into your subconscious and you will be able to apply them automatically without even thinking about them because they will already be in your sub-conscious mind. When you can literally do real estate investing while asleep is when it becomes easy. The most successful investors have automated their minds to think like investors. That comes with repetition.

HUMILITY

An investor must be humble. History made it known that there are many famous people who have failed due to pride and arrogance. Doing more listening than talking and being perceptive, removing one's ego, and endeavoring not to make assumptions are attributes of a humble person. A humble person doesn't get angry easily or get troubled. This means one has hugged changes, allow challenges, and come to know that everything cannot work out as intended.

You tend to learn from your mistakes and open your mind to new ideas when you are humble. People who think they already know everything have difficulty in embracing new ideas. Some call this behavior as having a full cup. Those with full cups fail woefully in real estate. When your cup is empty, you embrace new ideas and success is yours.

When you put blame on yourself for your shortcomings in business instead of putting it on others, it is called being humble. When you take responsibility for your successes and failures and have the mind of learning from them, you will become a successful investor.

Humility is an indication of strength and not weakness. You can be humble and yet still be a self-assured and bold leader. However, there is a thin line between pride and self-assurance, between being full of oneself and being sure of oneself. Successful investors are humble and self-assured.

TAKING ADVICE

Advice can be a very useful thing. Each person has an opinion. But to know who is right, the person who has already made exceptional results in a given field is usually the person that's mostly correct. The first few months are a very important and fragile time for beginners of real estate investment in their development. It is at this point that many good-intentioned family members, friends, and associates give their opinions. Beginners must not listen to the negative voice in their life. It may cause them to quit or pull back from giving it their full effort. To prevent the worse from happening, always seek your advice on a subject from a trustworthy source. If the person giving an advice on real estate has gained a complete fortune, you can listen to them. If not, do not ask for advice from such a person. Ensure the person who you want to seek the advice from is a reflection of someone you want to become. At times, people who tend to advise new investors on real estate business are those who have failed woefully at it. It may be a friend who has invested in it in the past and did not make anything from it. It may be a family member. Do not make the mistake of listening to them. The best people to get advice from are those who know about the business very well and very successful at it.

For instance, parents are regarded as a great choice for seeking advice on how to raise children. But if such parents were financially incapacitated throughout their lives, it will not be advisable taking advice from them on how to be financially capable because they have not experienced such a thing. We follow our parents' advice on things because that's how we were raised, even though they are not the most qualified to give us the advice in many fields, be it our career or finances. Most of us usually have that person we confide in for giving us good advice on things but do we think whether that person has what it takes investment-wise? We should be careful of taking advice from people that are financially incapacitated. Not taking their advice does not mean you are rude; you are just being careful and realistic.

Thus, ensure that those advising you on real estate investment are worthy of it. Make sure the person advising you is an expert in the field. If not, do not take the advice. Most times, people who are not experts give you bad advice. However, if a lawyer who is an expert in real estate investment advises you on the business, do not hesitate to take his advice because he definitely has the experience.

After making sure the person advising you is an expert, you need to know the reason why you are being given that advice. You should be able to know the perspective from which the person is advising you so as to know if it will help you in your endeavor or not. Take, for instance, the example of the real estate lawyer. Maybe at the time the lawyer is advising you, a new law is about to be enacted that affects the way he could advise his clients, so he will be hesitant in providing you the information you need. Another example may be an agent that tries to discourage you from buying a property because he wants to buy it himself, but just waiting for you to leave the idea of buying it.

The issue is similar to asking a barber whether you should get a haircut or not. Normally, the barber gets paid for the haircut, so you should expect he will answer in his favor, which means he will say "yes, you do need one" because he will be profiting from it.

That brings us to how to overcome getting bad advice from people that are expert in the field. The best solution is to make sure your interests go along with their interests. For example, if your lawyer knows that he will be getting paid as you close each real estate deal, he will make sure he does everything within his means to make it successful, by giving you good advice. Or if you compensate your real estate agent on every property he helps you in buying or reselling, he will make sure he does his best. People that are successful in real estate business make sure they align everybody's interest because, in the real world, people work very well when they know they have something to gain.

This is how our apprentice program was built, on mutually aligned interests. The profits are shared with us by our students 50/50. When they win, we also win. This gears our interest in giving them the best advice because our interests go hand in hand. When the student makes money, the mentors also make money.

We shall talk about the elephant in the room.

You probably believe by now that I am the greatest source for advice on real estate investment. But how will you know the advice I am dishing out is best for you?

Right techniques and strategies should be used by students to close deals; money is made when the students close a deal. My profits with my students depend on this book because it entails most precise advice on real estate investing. Proper foundation and right education are needed by my team so as to produce the best result because some of the readers of this book will go ahead to work with my team. That is how I have created all my courses, training, and articles; keeping the end in mind. The best of the best advice will be gotten from this book due to collectively-aligned interest. All my training, articles, and courses have been designed in this format.

WHO IS YOUR MENTOR?

There is no successful person without a mentor. We must know there is no self-made successful person. Every successful person has a mentor, or mentors, that have coached and trained the person. The natural effect of this is that it's the fastest shortcut to success. Having a mentor helps to speed up your success.

SUCCESSFUL REAL ESTATE INVESTORS HAVE MENTORS.

When choosing your mentor, choose wisely. Mostly the first person new investors meet is the one they tend to align with. Meanwhile, not having a mentor in real estate is the worst thing ever. Fortunately, figuring out the value of a mentor is not difficult. When taking advice, you will want to align yourself with people who are more successful and know better than you do about a subject as I have previously said. You should be able to determine the quality of a mentor by what they have personally achieved in real estate and also through the people they have mentored in the past. Do not allow someone who has never mentored anyone in the past to be your mentor even if they are greatly rich in their own right because mentoring is a skill unto itself. Be someone's mentee who has a good record for mentoring others into success. There is no time to be someone else's mentee guinea pig.

Choose a mentor sooner rather than later.

PARTNERS

Most investors take the usual step of adding on a partner to their inexperienced hustle when they first get started.

Mostly new investors want a partner because they do not want to invest alone, thinking their partner will bring a great value or the person is important to the job. Partnership is useful in business only if it is organized, and you partnered with the right person.

First of all, you should partner with someone for a specific period of time. It's common when two friends partner up in business, the timeframe for their partnership is not always specified and later when the unavoidable occurs, they will want the business to head in different directions. Unfortunately, they end up not going along well, and the business wavers. The best way to avoid this is that the partnership should have a timeframe from the onset.

Secondly, the partnership should be with someone providing a great value. A clash can occur in partnership when it's only one partner that's doing all the work or providing all the value, and the other partner is lazy and useless. To avoid this, ensure each partner brings value above and beyond just working in the business.

In addition, the role as well as the responsibilities of each partner should be made known to them.

In a business partnership, one must be ready to think about what's going to end the business although they may feel uneasy about it.

Ensure your partner is providing great value if you have already engaged yourself in a partnership. Put up a timeframe for the partnership to end, and draw a plan for who is going to be accountable or responsible for whatever happens. If your partner is not in line with this, then you are likely to have an unsuitable partner.

CHAPTER 4

SOURCES OF INCOME FROM REAL ESTATE INVESTMENT

When property and stocks are compared by experts, the comparisons are only occasionally correct. Their belief mostly is that property yields only one source of return that is significant: potential gains in price. The claim by the book named 'Winning the Loser's Game' by Charles Ellis deduces that, "Over the past 20 years, home prices have gone lower than the consumer price index and have returned lower than Treasury bills. Therefore, owning residential real estate is not exactly a great investment."

Putting aside the source and how Ellis came up with his long-term house price figures for a while—no statistics have shown that housing, comparative to incomes or Consumer Price Index, has become cheaper—Ellis (and other finance/economics types) outrageously misunderstands how total potential returns that property offers should be measured by investors. At least 20 other sources of financial returns were neglected by Ellis by which the investors can generate income from their portfolio of properties.

When it comes to property evaluation, you should certainly weigh the possibilities for price gains, but also go further. Even with no gain in price, you can acquire double-digit rates of return (and much more sometimes) from your investments in property.

Deciding which sources of returns best align with your investment goals is up to you—and correspondingly, for every property you assess, which sources of return appear doable. Properties that present a total range of possibilities are few. Apply each test of possibility to every property you consider to fully see the potential. Multiple sources of returns are presented by each property.

WILL THERE BE PRICE GAINS WHEN THE PROPERTY APPRECIATES?

Many people do not differentiate price gains that come from appreciation and those that are as a result of inflation in everyday speech. When demand grows faster than supply, appreciation happens for a particular type of property and/or location. Inflation has the tendency to increase prices —regardless of whether demand and supply remain in balance.

During the past 15 to 20 years, Central London, San Francisco's Pacific Heights, and Brooklyn's Williamsburg neighborhood homes have experienced uncommonly high rates of appreciation. And just since 1990, basically due to the fact that UF students and faculty alike now strongly have a preference for "walk or bike to campus" locations, homes within a few miles of the University of Florida campus have increased three times the market price.

Areas vary in their appreciation rate. A few neighborhoods in Detroit have suffered significant decrease in value, although properties situated in Williamsburg and Pacific Heights have increased in value to rates much higher than the increase in the Consumer Price Index (CPI). Appreciation does not happen randomly. Appreciation potential can be forecasted.

In a like manner, you do not need to get caught in the serious and long-term down-drafts that plague urban communities and neighborhoods that lose their jobs' economic base. Just as different socioeconomic elements point to right time, right place, right cost, similar indicators can signal wrong time, wrong place, and wrong cost.

Appreciation is not needed. Would it be a good idea for you to regularly invest in properties situated in areas heading for above-average appreciation? Not really. In the remaining part of this chapter, I will show you many ways you can make profit with property. A few investors possess rental properties in deteriorating areas—yet they are able to build a multimillion-dollar net worth. My initial properties constantly yielded cash flows like a slot machine payoff but did not gain a lot from price increases (inflation or appreciation).

If your choice is a fast money, flip and fix strategy, appreciation doesn't mean much either. Additionally, when you buy at a value 10 to 30 percent lower than the market value, you earn an instant appreciation that is not identified with market temperature. Discard the inclination to believe that you can't earn good money with property except when its market price increases in value.

WILL THERE BE AN INCREASE IN PRICE GAIN FROM INFLATION?

The oft-cited Yale economist, Robert Shiller, in his book, Irrational Exuberance, makes the conclusion that houses perform poorly as investments. Going by his reckoning, since 1948, the genuine (inflation-adjusted) price growth in housing is around 1—at best 2—percent on the average each year.

"Regardless of whether this $16,000 house sold in 2004," says the noteworthy professor, "at a cost of $360,000, it does not imply incredible returns on this investment still ... a real (i.e., inflation-adjusted) yearly rate of increment of a little below 2 percent a year."

Shiller does not think like an investor but as an economist. Each investor wants to shield his wealth from the destructive influence of sudden inflation. Even if we acknowledge Shiller's numbers—and I trust them as reasonable, though surely not beyond critique—the data demonstrates that real estate has kept investors outside the effects of inflation every decade for over 75 years.

For stocks (or bonds), this is not true. Consider the most

inflationary time in the history of U.S: 1966–1982. In 1966, a house's median price equaled $25,000; the Dow Jones Index hit 1,000. The CPI jumped from 100 to 300 during the following eighteen years. In 1982, a house's median price had gone up to $72,000; the DJIA closed the year at 780—it's lowest in 18 years.

Inflation Risk: As compared to stocks, property protects your investment better. Nobody is aware of what the future holds. Will the CPI begin climbing at a steeper pace once again? The U.S. government at the runaway rate prints cash and floats new debt, the odds point toward that direction. During times of accelerating inflation, a great number of people would rejoice at just remaining even.

Imagine that you were a true blue "stocks for retirement" type of investor in the early to mid-1960s—and you were 45 years of age then. As you approach age 65, in 1982, your inflation-adjusted net worth sits at possibly 30 percent of the amount you had planned and hoped for. What do you do in this situation? Continue the job for another 10 years? Sell off the homestead and downsize? Borrow cash from a rich friend of yours who has investment in real estate?

Indexes and averages are not bought by property investors. Economists calculate in the nether land of averages and aggregates. Investors purchase particular properties in accordance with their personal investment objectives. The actual price gains (inflation in addition to appreciation) that real investors earn are not captured by an economist's average.

No investor who chooses properties intelligently for their wealth-building potential picks such properties at random. If you have desire to outperform the average price increment of real estate— despite the fact that the averages themselves look quite great— you absolutely can.

EARN GOOD PROFIT FROM CASH FLOWS

Income property yields (unleveraged) cash flows of 5 to 12 percent typically unlike the overwhelming majority of stocks. You can earn $50,000 to $120,000 yearly if you possess a $1,000,000 property free and clear of financing. You might earn cash flows (dividend payments) of $15,000 to $30,000 yearly if you owned a $1,000,000 portfolio of stocks.

The largest source of return for unleveraged properties has originated from cash flow historically. Own income properties if you desire to grow a passive stream of income that is protected from inflation.

INCREASE YOUR PROFIT MARGIN WITH LEVERAGE

Financial analysts, know-nothing economists, and different media-anointed specialists make claims that price gains from property give real (inflation-adjusted) returns of about one to two percent yearly. In doing such, they exclude the return-boosting power of OPM (other people's money—normally, mortgage financing).

Low price rates gain creates great returns. Let us assume you acquire a property worth $100,000. You borrow $80,000 and put $20,000 down. During the subsequent five years, the CPI progresses by 50 percent. However, your property lagged the CPI. Its cost increased by 25 percent only. Your real wealth decreased, right? No, it increased actually.

You presently own a property that is worth $125,000, but your equity wealth— your initial $20,000 cash equity in the property— has risen to $45,000 (not including mortgage amortization of principal). You have more than increased your money by double. To have even remained with the CPI, your equity only needed to increase to $30,000.

The U.K., Asia, and majority of Europe's yields often fall somewhat below the yield available throughout the US.

Acorns into Oak Trees. Because it grows acorns (small upfront payments) into clear and free properties worth many multiples of the initial measure of cash invested, investing in real estate builds wealth. Let's return to that Shiller example.

In 1948, the homebuyer paid the amount of $16,000. Did the homebuyer pay in cash? Unlikely. Ten to 20 percent down set the standard—say, 20 percent or $3,600 (0.2 × $16,000). At Shiller's theoretical 2004 value of $360,000, the homebuyer increased his original investment 100 times over. The homeowner enjoyed a 50-fold increment of his $3,600 upfront payment even if we say the 2004 property value comes in at a value of $180,000.

What about stock gains during the 1948 to 2004 period? The DJIA hovered around 200 in 1948 (by the way, still around 40 percent beneath its 1929 peak of 360). The DJIA remained at about 8,000 in 2004—a 40-fold gain. Not awful, but still lower than the profits from property (and a whole lot less when cash flows are brought into the comparison with returns). [Note: As at mid-2009, the DJIA sits at about 8,000—whereas property costs (in all but the most distressed zones) are still up from 2004 and far up from 1998, the year that the DJIA initially hit 8,000.]

USE LEVERAGE TO INCREASE PROFIT FROM CASH FLOWS

Investors do not just magnify their equity gains from leverage traditionally, they likewise magnify their cash flows return rates. You pay $1,000,000 cash for an apartment that yields a 7.5 percent net income (after all operating costs, no financing). Not terrible. But if you finance $800,000 of the $1,000,000 purchase cost at, say, 30 years, 5.75 percent interest, you invest only $200,000 in cash. Your net income measures up to $75,000 (.075 × 1,000,000) and your yearly mortgage payments (debt service) will add up to around $56,000. You take $19,000 ($75,000 less $56,000). Your cash flow return has been boosted (called cash on cash) to 9.5 percent from 7.5 percent (19,000 ÷ 200,000).

WEALTH BUILDING THROUGH AMORTIZATION

Assume that your $1,000,000 property throws off zero cash flows. Every dollar of net operating income is applied in paying down your $800,000 mortgage balance. You own the property free and clear after a period of twenty years. This property is still worth $1,000,000; it experienced no gain in price.

No price gains from appreciation, no price gains from inflation, and no money earned from cash flows. A little bit pessimistic and unrealistic, right? Yet, over a period of 20-years, you grew your equity to $1,000,000 from $200,000—a gain of five-fold and an annual compound growth rate in excess of 8 percent.

Your tenants just purchased a $1,000,000 property for you. That's the reason I tell my students, "Rent or purchase?" is an inappropriate question. All inhabitants buy—the appropriate question is one of ownership. You still pay your landlord his mortgage if you rent. Your landlord receives the benefits of ownership—while tenants bear the expenses. It appears to me a great deal for property investors.

RETURNS FROM RENTS GO UP OVER TIME

Most property owners increase their rents. Possibly not this year. Maybe not one year from now. But over a five-year or more period, increasing rents results in increasing cash flows. Demand will drive rents up as more individuals want to live in the neighborhood where your property is situated if you've chosen an appropriate time, appropriate place, and appropriate price location. Or on the other hand, inflationary pressures increase rents as government pumps paper money into the economy. You gain either way. In fact, even if inflationary jumps in your expenses are not matched by your rent increases, you can gain.

Let's go back to our apartment building example. Gross rent collections amount to $125,000; mortgage payments amount to $56,000; net operating income amount to $75,000; your cash flow amount to $19,000.

Gross rents	$125,000
Annual mortgage payments	56,000
Net operating income	75,000
Vacancy and expenses	50,000
Cash flow	19,000

Firstly, let's assume that both your rents and expenses increase by 8 percent.

Below are the revised amounts:

Gross rents	$135,000
Annual mortgage payments	56,000
Net operating income	81,000
Vacancy and expenses	54,000
Cash flow	25,000

Your cash flow is boosted by 31 percent following an 8 percent increase in rents and expenses:

$25,000 \div 19,000 = 1.31$

If expenses had risen by 12 percent and rents increased mildly by only 6 percent per year (p.a.), your cash flow would still increase:

Gross rents	$132,500
Annual mortgage payments	56,000
Net operating income	76,500
Vacancy and expenses	56,000
Cash flow	20,500

$$20,500 \div 19,000 = 1.08$$

[NB: You can run various scenarios with these numbers and other numbers introduced all through this chapter. Results are not guaranteed. You will both estimate and make the potential returns for the properties you purchase through your very own market and entrepreneurial analysis.

But I do urge you to envision the return possibilities that property investing offers realistically. At that point, as you assess properties, markets, and the economic outlook for your geographic zones of interest, figure out the probabilities. Which sources of return appear to be the most promising? Which sources of return appear to be remote? What risks could make the applecart upset?

REFINANCING TO INCREASE CASH FLOWS

Your cash flows increase when you increase your rents (or your expenses decrease). In addition, you increase your cash flows when you refinance to reduce your annual mortgage payments. A future refinancing at rates lower than those available at present appears somewhat remote today.

Be that as it may, who knows? Beginning from 1925 until the late 1950s, interest rates on long-term mortgages were in the range of 4.0 and 5.0 percent. A 6.5 percent, 30-year loan, refinanced into a

4.5 percent, a 30-year loan would not just cut off your mortgage payments by 20 percent, it would also increase your cash flows by a significantly higher percentage.

We may again confront mortgage interest rates of 8 to 10 percent in some future time. A later refinance at reduced interest rates becomes ever more likely under those market conditions.

REFINANCING TO POCKET CASH

Except history makes a U-turn, purchase a property today and within 10 to 15 years, you can have it sold for 50 to 100 percent more than the amount you paid. You gain a huge pile of money. But what if selling is not what you want to do? Will you still be able to get your hands on a portion of that equity that you have built up? This is possible beyond doubt. Simply organize a cash-out refinance.

Here's the way this possible source of return functions. Say your $1 million property is presently worth $1.5 million after 10 years. You've made down payments of your loan balance to $650,000. Your equity has risen to $850,000 from $200,000 ($1.5 million less $650,000). You get a new 80 percent loan-to-value ratio mortgage of $1.2 million. You get away with $550,000 tax-free!

But don't spend that money. Reinvest the cash. Purchase another income property. Yes, you presently owe monthly mortgage payments on your initial property that is higher, and your property will reduce in cash flow. But your total cash flows will increase with the extra cash flows from your second property. How's that for having your cake and eating it as well?

PURCHASING AT BELOW-MARKET PRICE

When the economists (mis)calculate the profits that property investors get, they discard the fact that savvy buyers frequently acquire incredible properties for lower than their market worth. Opportunity (grass-is-greener) merchants, don't-want vendors, poorly educated sellers, incompetent sellers, sellers that lack knowledge—and in today's markets most importantly—financially upset sellers, will all sell at below-market costs.

The financially stressed and distressed today are not only inclusive of individual property owners but also the mortgage lenders themselves unlike in normal times. Financial companies now own foreclosures (called REOs) in excess of a million that they must sell off as fast as lining up buyers to take these properties off their books is possible.

How do you find and purchase these properties for lower than they are worth? You'll discover this in subsequent part of this book series.

SELLING AT A PRICE ABOVE MARKET VALUE

How do you sell a property for a price higher than market value? Look for a buyer that is not knowledgeable, not competent, or pressed by time. Offer seller financing, a wraparound, or maybe a lease option. Develop your promotion and negotiation skills. Match the exceptional features and advantages of the property. Sell the property with an interest rate that is below market rate assumable (or subject-to) loan.

On few occasions, buyers pay a higher amount than market value because they don't have an idea of (or care less) what they're doing. Few times they pay more to get a much-wanted feature or terms of purchase/financing. Whatever reason they have, if you have a desire to exploit this possibility, you've made another source of return.

PROPERTY VALUE CREATION THROUGH SMARTER MANAGEMENT

You increase your rent collections (without necessarily increasing your rents) when you deal with your properties and your tenants much more intelligently; you lessen tenant turnover; prospect conversions increases; you spend less money, yet spend more effectively for capital replacements, maintenance, and promotion. You enjoy pleasant, peaceful, and beneficial relations with the tenants.

Luckily for you, most investor-sized rental properties' owners (in opposition to institutional-size) manage their investments poorly. Why is this fortunate? This is because their mal-management gives you opportunities. You can implement a more effective and competitive management system to increase the cash flows of the property and lift its market value simultaneously upon acquiring a property.

CREATING VALUE WITH A SAVVY MARKET STRATEGY

Despite the fact that investors tend to manage their properties ineffectively, as savvy marketers, they demonstrate even less skill. Go to websites of some properties. Navigate through to a sample of listings. Take a look at the listing promotional information provided. Peruse the property photos. Does the agent tell a persuasive tale about the property? Is the sales message one that positions that property against the numerous competing properties that likewise strive for attention? Do the photos of appropriate-ties disclose a well-cared-for property—a property that is inviting enough to tenants to call it home?

I will provide you with the answers. No! No! No! Its implication? Additional opportunities for you to gain a competitive advantage. You earn higher cash flows; you give your tenants a better home; and when an opportunity to sell comes up, your property will command a higher price when you incorporate the management knowledge and marketing strategy lessons (which would be discussed in subsequent parts of this book series).

CREATING VALUE BY IMPROVING THE LOCATION

A famous cliché´ in real estate goes, "You can transform anything about a property asides from its location." True or false?

Completely false. Not only can you enhance a location, but doing so additionally provides one of your most powerful sources of return.

Take a minute to think. What does the idea of location include? What makes the location of your house desirable or undesirable? Aesthetics, accessibility, good public transportation, tranquility, the people who live in the neighborhood, cleanliness, parks, schools, nightlife, shopping... the list could go on. What's the ideal approach to enhance some or all of these attributes? Community action. Instances abound throughout the United States and also around the world.

UNIT RENTALS TO UNIT OWNERSHIP CONVERSION

Purchase wholesale, sell retail. A grocer purchases a 48-can box of tomato soup and after that sells each can separately at an increased retail price. A similar wholesale-to-retail methodology can be implemented by property investors.

Purchase a 48-unit apartment building; then, on completion of documentation and lawful approvals, sell each apartment separately. In principle, you can apply a similar condo-conversion methodology to mobile home parks, office buildings, hotels, marinas, boat storage facilities neighborhood strip centers, self-storage warehouse units, private aircraft hangars, and other kinds of rental real estate where potential clients may have a preference to own than to rent. In each situation, you typically pay less per unit (or psf) for a whole building than retail buyers want to pay for the smaller amount of room that they require to meet their needs.

There are never constant opportunities for conversion profits. Potential profit margins swing between "make an easy million" to "call the bankruptcy lawyer" as property markets change.

Monitor the relative per-unit costs of space sold in smaller sizes to end users and properties sold as rentals (income property investments) to capitalize on this source of return.

LOWER-VALUE USE TO HIGHER-VALUE USE CONVERSION

You may benefit from reverse conversions in such upset market conditions. Purchase a fractured condo and operate the condo as a rental property.

Let's assume that in your area, single-family residential (SFR) space rents at $2 per square foot (psf) due to a severe shortage, and offices rent at $1 psf due to abundance of supply. Five years from the present time, SFR rents at $1.50 psf due to the abundance of overbuilding, and office space rents at $3.00 psf due to job and strong economic growth. What may you do if zoning permits? Convert your SFR into offices.

Typically, conversion of use needs you to revamp (to some degree at least) the old, lower-value space use to match the market needs of the higher-value use. However, when relative costs and/or rent levels gradually grows wider, conversion of use can create a lucrative source of profit.

SUBDIVISION OF YOUR BUNDLE OF PROPERTY RIGHTS

You actually own an extensive bundle of divisible property rights when a freehold estate is yours. Such rights may be inclusive of (but are not constrained to):

- Air

- Coal

- Mineral

- Water

- Oil and gas

- Subsurface

- Access

- Leasehold

- Development

- Timber

- Grazing

- Easement

- Solar/sunlight

Numerous nearby property owners stashed away several million dollars when Donald Trump erected his United Nations World Tower. Why? Trump paid these owners to give him a portion of their air rights. Instead of 40 stories, The City of New York granted Trump permission to construct 80 stories, as the zoning law then specified after acquiring their air rights.

When in Hong Kong, you'll observe that skyscrapers tower directly above some of the MTR stations. The Hong Kong government was paid by developers for the privilege to utilize that airspace— despite the fact that government retained ownership and use rights of the land below the apartment buildings.

Almost everybody understands that to earn revenues, property owners can sell leasehold rights. (Not every government, however, allow leaseholds for all properties—and when they do, they may constrain the terms and cost of the leasehold agreement severely). In addition to leasehold, however, you might lease, sell, or license other rights that derive from a freehold estate. Another source of return can be created by transferring one or more of these other rights.

SUBDIVISION OF SPACE (THE PHYSICAL PROPERTY)

Condominium conversions stand for one form of subdividing in one sense. But more often than not, subdividing is referred to as leasing or selling buildings or land in smaller parcels, most commonly, a developer who purchases 500 acres and cuts it up and sells half-acre lots off to homebuilders. In another instance, consider a closed down Kmart store. A still-flourishing big box retailer may pay $10 per square foot to let out the entire now-empty building.

A real estate business person could master lease the property instead, and subdivide the interior space into an assortment of uses such as offices, childcare, as well as smaller retail merchants. Every small tenant pays a higher price per square foot (ppsf) rent rate than would the Best Buy who might probably lease the entire building. The entrepreneur may subdivide a portion of the parking lot area for additional retail/restaurant uses in the event that the new space users need lower parking ratios than the old Kmart.

Thoughtful entrepreneurs with deep knowledge of the market and possibility thinking are consistently on the outlook for properties to subdivide. The sum of the parts surpasses the value when viewed as a whole in such instances.

CREATE ASSEMBLAGE (OR PLOTTAGE) VALUE

When smaller parcels are combined into a larger parcel of space or land, you create plottage or assemblage value. Let's assume you discover an ideal site to construct a new neighborhood shopping center, at least four acres is required by zoning and planners for such a development. The site amounts to four acres but eight different people own it in one-half acre lots. The lots are worth $10,000 each individually—or $80,000 altogether.

As a four-acre shopping site, however, the land would sell for a price of $250,000. Now you see how to make a good profit. Persuade each of the present owners to sell off his lot to you at its present market value (or even at a value that sits to some degree above market value). Maybe the Walt Disney Company was the champion assembler to make plottage value. Over a time-range of 10 years, 25 square miles of Central Florida land was secretly accumulated by Disney at agricultural-valued prices. The value of the aggregate site most likely surpassed cost by a factor of 20 (or more) once they finished this assemblage.

ACQUIRE DEVELOPMENT/REDEVELOPMENT RIGHTS

Go back to the example of the four-acre neighborhood shopping center. You achieve success. You secured all eight lots at a total price of $130,000 (many of those owners did not want to sell—so you improved your offer). Can you begin constructing the center? No. first, you must obtain a long list of government permits and approvals. In this manner, your current site value of $250,000 stands independent of a government go-ahead.

The land could command a $500,000 cost with permits available. You could take your profit by selling now. Or you could remain in the game. Spend $50,000 (or around that) for lawyers, public hearings, soil tests, traffic studies, environmental clearance, and anything else the city powers toss at you. For the permit process (with luck—and no unexpected delays), a period of 6 months to 12 months is required. You earn an extra $200,000 if everything goes as planned.

Government endorsements add to a property's value in real estate. It is a property that is ripe for development, renovation, redevelopment, conversion—or destruction. Acquire those necessary permits, and you earn a return that is decent-sized.

TAX SHELTER YOUR CAPITAL PROFITS AND PROPERTY INCOME

Shield your income and capital gains from the government's insatiable grasp to build wealth. Luckily (under current tax law), real estate investments give you more opportunity to abstain from paying taxes than any other asset class.

All (or almost all) of your positive cash flow is sheltered by depreciation (noncash) deductions. As you pyramid your investment properties, a Section 1231 exchange protects your capital gain. From the sales of your personal residence(s), the $250,000/$500,000 capital gain exclusion gives you tax-free gains. Tax-free cash is deposited into your bank account by a cash-out refinance (which will be repaid for you by your tenants). And if you purchase a "first-time" home, the recently authorized $8,000 tax credit makes provision for part (or possibly all) of the money for your down payment.

Some naïve souls may make objections. "I can build my stock market wealth free of tax through my 401(k), 403(b), and IRA plans. Property is beaten by that tax break."

Well, even if the property was beaten by that tax break—which it doesn't—you fail to remember that the government will tax each penny as ordinary income when you start to draw on that cash during retirement. Additionally, the IRS will get 35 to 50 percent of those sums (taxes plus penalties) if you want to take advantage of that cash kitty prior to reaching age 59-1/2 (as almost 50 percent of Americans do). The IRS still reaches in and grabs its own share if you die before withdrawal.

Buy investment real estate to limit income and wealth loss to the IRS.

DIVERSIFY FROM FINANCIAL ASSETS

Although a few investors have a preference for stocks, those investors would prove themselves wise to extend some portion of their portfolio into property.

Property costs have kept pace with or surpassed the growth rate in the CPI as investment experience demonstrates during times of anticipated and unexpected inflation. Even better, leverage changes little price gains into double-digit rates of increment in your equity wealth.

When compared to stock and bond prices, property prices demonstrate much less volatility. Compared to the precipitous periodic drops in stock prices of stocks, the ongoing depression, surfeit of foreclosures, and costs downturns for many properties appear to be mild. Even in the difficult times property markets, costs have only fallen back to their 2004-2005 levels. All major stock indices sit below their levels of 1998 as I write.

Most financial planners today encourage asset diversification. Historical experience as well as ongoing experience support that view. The mantra "stocks, stocks, and more stocks for retirement" does not meet the test of experience. Include property to your investments—if not for its superior gains, then to lessen your portfolio risks.

CHAPTER 5

IS PROPERTY ALWAYS BEST?

A few individuals think that I serve as head cheerleader for real estate investment. They are correct in one sense. More average individuals have built sizeable measures of wealth through property than some other kind of savings or investment as records have shown.

I do not say that "Property investments will beat stocks or bonds any time, any place, at any cost" however. I told my investor audiences that I would not purchase property in the then-current hotspots, for instance, Las Vegas, Miami, Singapore, Dublin, or Dubai as early as 2005. Those markets were driven by speculative frenzy—not by reasoned fundamental evaluation of risks and rewards.

So, as people often do, when they ask me that "Which investment type provides the best returns —real estate or stock?" I give the reply, "It all depends." In 1989, I would have rather invested in the S&P 500 index fund than Tokyo real estate certainly. I would have had a preference for the DJIA to property in Berlin in 1993. I would rather have purchased Apple Computer stock over a Hong Kong condo situated on the Peak in 1997.

You have to depend on investment and market analysis. Generally, investors do not make more profit with property than they do with stocks. I have never said something different. However, that begs the question, "Which investment offers the best probabilities and possibilities this day?"

Given today's bargain property cost relative to where property values will probably stand 6 to 10 years from the present; given the fact you can build huge increases in property wealth (equity) without huge gains in cost; given the relative income yields of stocks (or bonds) vs property; given the property's tax advantages relative to all other investments; given the various sources of returns that property offers; and last—but not the least—given the entrepreneurial abilities that you can apply to property to make its cost and cash flows increase; then, yes, in the present day's market, I will lead the cheers for having real estate investments willingly.

MANAGE AND MARKET YOUR PROPERTIES MORE PROFITABLY

A lot of people have the belief that small-time business owners mismanage rental spaces and properties. This is true. There are so many reasons why this is correct. Amongst them are laziness, failure to key up with changes in the market, failure to make the much-needed improvement to their properties, and the failure to develop a sound master plan of target marketing.

On the whole, these common failures mean you can certainly increase your gains from properties simply by marketing and managing them very effectively. Effective management requires less time and effort which is an added bonus to you.

PROTECT YOUR PROFITS FROM THE IRS (TAX SHELTER)

In order to build wealth and be assured of some levels of financial security, there is the need to protect your gains and profits from the greedy arms of the government. Luckily, income tax laws allow property owners to skip taxation in at least four important ways:

SERIAL HOME SELLERS

A good number of Americans profit, tax-free, from investments made in their homes. This is the way it works.

On the whole, when you own an investment property, payments

are made by you for capital gains tax on your resale profits at the moment you sell it. When reselling your personal residence, however, your profits are received by you, absolutely tax-free, up to $250,000 ($500,000 for couples). So long as you've resided in that property for two of the last five years, you are not compelled by any law to mention this profit to the IRS.

It even gets better; you are allowed to repeat this purchase and sale every two years. In an ideal world, you search for a home with great fix-up and renovation potential, pay for it, create value for it, sell it again, and reinvest those tax-free proceeds in more properties. Feel free to continue this process until you attain your desired level of financial freedom or till you get tired of moving. For singles or childless couples, serial home ownership proves to be a perfect way of making fast (when compared to means) and task-free gains. Put your kids to work and get them involved if you have any. They stand to learn extremely valuable lessons in real estate renovating and investing.

SECTION 1031 EXCHANGES

You can also sell your investment properties tax-free in addition to buying and selling a series of personal residences without paying taxes. All that is needed of you is to adhere to guidelines placed in Section 1031 of the Internal Revenue Code. Expert Realty professionals could help in setting up important paperwork needed to execute these tax-free "exchanges". Notice how the word "exchanges" is placed in quotations because the term is actually inappropriate. You are not required to trade this property with another owner. Just sell off one property and pay for another one within a space of months.

DEPRECIATION

The IRS taxes your net annual earnings in most businesses. However, when you own rental properties, you can actually protect (shelter) a great deal of your cash flow from taxation by making use of a non-cash tax deduction called depreciation. Let's say your apartment building, excluding the value of the land, is worth an estimated $500,000. Pretax cash earnings from that property is equivalent to $20,000 per year. Having said that, you won't pay taxes on that $20,000 of income. Taxes are paid only on $1,950 ($20,000 of income less $18,150 for allowable depreciation). If probably, your rental property yields just $10,000 annually in pretax cash income, one might ask, what becomes of that $18,150 deduction for depreciation? In this case, you could write off (deduct) the $8,150($18,150 depreciation less $10,000 property income) of unused "loss" from the taxable sums you receive from other taxable earnings (business profits, wages, dividends, and interest).

TAX-DEFERRED RETIREMENT PLANS

Are you the owner of an IRA retirement? If that's your case, you could invest part of it, or better still, all of it all in real estate.

Sadly, most people believe in investing these retirement funds in corporate America's bonds, stocks, money market accounts, or mutual funds. This is not correct! In his book, IRA Wealth: Revolutionary IRA Strategies for Real Estate Investment (page 3), Patrick Rice explains in full these real estate investing methods. This is what rice has to say:

After the sharp decline of the stock market, many could only stand by and watch as their retirement savings lost their accumulated value. Not many investors realized that there was another path which offered safety and growth together. That other path is none other than real estate.......contrary to popular opinion, it is possible and absolutely legal to hold real estate in an IRA account-and to reap unprecedented returns.

If you have piled up funds in a tax-favored retirement plan, you are hereby urged to talk with a financial pro or study subsequent books in this series. Most likely, you will find in it a brilliant idea, on how to diversify at least part of your IRA savings into real estate. IRA funds invested in real estate grows, tax-free within that account exactly the same way bonds, stocks and CDS would.

TAXES: SUMMING UP

Tax laws have proven to be too complex for me to itemize and break into details in this beginners' book on investing in realty. However, be thankful of the reality that, to a large extent, you can shelter your realty proceeds from the IRS.

As this series on real estate investment unfolds, I will stick to revealing to you how to make tons of money in real estate. To complement this, I will show you how to stash away the profits without giving away a pod chunk of that money to the tax collectors.

DISCOUNTED NOTES, TAX DEEDS, TAX LIENS, AND REALTY STOCKS

You've been meaning to make it big in realty without the hassles of managing tenants or lifting any paintbrush? Consider then, the high returns of dealing in discounted notes and mortgages.

THE BASICS OF DISCOUNTED NOTES

It has become a common occurrence for sellers of investment properties to take back some or all of their buyer's purchase price (owner finance). Monthly payments are then made by buyers to the sellers directly.

A seller may decide he or she wants cash against the monthly payments, after a period of time. In order to get this cash, the seller (the note holder) sells off the note to some other investor-normally for a price lesser than the amount on the note owed by the buyers of the original note-holders property.

Take as an instance, I sell a property to you and take back a mortgage note for $25,000. The remaining balance on the note reduces to, say, $21,500, after some years. I need cash. In order to attract an investor to buy this note, it's likely I would sell it for $17,500.

You would be wondering, "Why sell for just $17,500?" That's how this market works. Noteholders who wish to attract an investor must accept a discount.

HOW MUCH IS THIS DISCOUNT? IT ALL DEPENDS ON SOME FACTORS.

Understand clearly that tens of thousands of investors in the United States today are raking in wonderful reruns in realty. You can join them if you want to.

TAX LIENS AND TAX DEEDS.

When property owners and real estate investors fail to pay property taxes, the local government places a tax lien against the property. The Government sells the property through a tax deed if the taxes remain not cleared. In subsequent books, I'll give an infomercial to reveal to investors the ways they can make money while purchasing these tax liens and tax deeds. Although it's never as easy and risk-free, from the moment you learn your area rules and procedures, earning tens of thousands of dollars every year by dealing in these government-issued certificates becomes a piece of cake.

STOCKS OF REITS AND HOMEBUILDERS

It's strongly advisable to directly own and manage real estate. Getting involved directly in the realty market is a guarantee that you will earn more than passive investors in stock exchange by a long shot. Notwithstanding, here's another alternative, buy stocks issued by real estate investment trusts REITs and big Homebuilders like Toll Brothers, Lennar, WPP, and K&B. REITs are those companies that manage and own big properties like office buildings, apartment complexes, shop centers, and warehouses.

Sometime after the general stock market downturn in early 2000,

Homebuilders and REITs stocks continued to mark positive total returns of 10 to 25 percent every year. Again, unlike the stocks of some companies, REIT stocks pay a 6 to 9 percent cash dividends every year.

Investors who wish to build a fortune in stocks are encouraged to own shares in several REITs and Homebuilders at the very least. These are companies who don't only offer good returns, they reduce the total danger of your investment portfolio. It is the duty of real estate stocks to diversify your holdings of bonds and stocks.

Passive income investments are not for the faintest of hearts. It is for those who desire more freedom, enough time, and a financially stable retirement. In relation to realty, passive income refers to the buying of properties or several properties and placing the units up for lease as a means of receiving a monthly cash flow. If you can charge more in rent than a combination of your maintenance costs, mortgage, and other expenses, you stand to live off the said cash flow.

CONCLUSION

Attaining financial security through investments in realty is more than just a plan to fantasize about during your lunch break at your 9 to 5 job. Turning this dream into a reality prepares you for an early retirement. In order to do this, cleanse yourself and your thoughts from the common notions of wealth and money. Should you insist on following what you were told is the standard route to wealth, then you are fast approaching a dead end.

Financial security is nothing about being confined in a cycle of slaving for money, piling it up, and praying that one day this money delivers protection. You've been led to believe that piling your hard-earned money in a 401k, IRA, stocks, or annuities will someday grant you that privilege to live a hedonistic life and bother no more about your finances. Recent records have proven that this doesn't work. Investments in realty is a different story, however.

In order to attain financial security, think first about investing in real estate. Are you still asking what makes investing in real estate the correct path towards attaining a fortune? This should answer your question. For beginners, you can start with little risk and little or no cash while sticking to your full-time job. Second, rental realty provides you with a flow of passive income every month which eases you slowly from the clutches of that stress-filled 9 to 5 job. Third, it's easy to control the equity in your properties to purchase more rental units or to finance other businesses that provide an automatic and a lasting source of income.

Sitting down, folding your arms, and crossing your fingers, while hoping to arrive at that mythological destination called "someday" is no way for anyone to live his/her life. Sadly, majority of people live their lives this way. Trapped and distressed is how they feel, while they long all day to taste that financial security they've been dreaming about. With the soundest of values, you have been equipped to take the right action today by investing in real estate and grasping that fortune you've always hoped for sooner or later. It allows your money to work for you instead of vice-versa.

Best Regards,
Investing Money & Mastery
www.investingmoneymastery.com

FREE ONLINE TRAINING

Thank you for reading this book. As a way of showing my appreciation, I want to give you a **3 Day Training program absolutely FREE** along with this book.

Free Training Reveals Step-By-Step...

How To Make Fortunes With Real Estate Investing

[Visualize The Feeling of Being Financially Free]

This free training concisely covers everything you need to know regarding how to find; assess; buy below market value; renovate; & sell properties for maximum profit in any market condition.

http://bit.ly/real_estate_training

Go to the above url to access your free training.

43274162R00037

Made in the USA
Lexington, KY
26 June 2019